Contents

Driving dogs

The Kennel Club's Pastoral group is made up of 37 dog breeds. Pastoral dogs are skilled and hardworking. These dogs were first developed to drive animals, such as sheep, reindeer and cattle. The dogs worked with ranchers to move large flocks or herds from one area to another. They would run frantically, bark aggressively and nip at the animals' heels to move them forward.

Many pastoral dogs have also become popular as pets. These smart dogs enjoy being useful. Whether they are competing in an organized activity or learning commands in their own back garden, they take their jobs seriously. Many breeds have a strong desire to please their owners.

Because of their high energy levels, pastoral dogs aren't for everyone. They can be loud and boisterous. Some will even try to herd small children if they have nothing else to do. Owners must provide these dogs with plenty of activity.

Pastoral dogs come in a wide range of sizes and coat types. From the small Corgi to the giant Old English Sheepdog, pastoral-dog lovers are bound to find a breed that is right for them.

Collies, Corgis and Other
PASTORAL DOGS

by Tammy Gagne

raintree

Raintree is an imprint of Capstone Global Library Limited, a company incorporated in England and Wales having its registered office at 264 Banbury Road, Oxford, OX2 7DY – Registered company number: 6695582

www.raintree.co.uk
myorders@raintree.co.uk

Text © Capstone Global Library Limited 2017
The moral rights of the proprietor have been asserted.

Edited by Alesha Halvorson
Designed by Terri Poburka
Picture research by Kelly Garvin
Production by Katy LaVigne

ISBN 978 1 4747 2084 7 (hardback)
20 19 18 17 16
10 9 8 7 6 5 4 3 2 1

ISBN 978 1 4747 2098 4 (paperback)
21 20 19 18 17
10 9 8 7 6 5 4 3 2 1

British Library Cataloguing in Publication Data
A full catalogue record for this book is available from the British Library.

Every effort has been made to contact copyright holders of material reproduced in this book. Any omissions will be rectified in subsequent printings if notice is given to the publisher.

All the internet addresses (URLs) given in this book were valid at the time of going to press. However, due to the dynamic nature of the internet, some addresses may have changed, or sites may have changed or ceased to exist since publication. While the author and publisher regret any inconvenience this may cause readers, no responsibility for any such changes can be accepted by either the author or the publisher.

Acknowledgements
Corbis: Asa Lindholm/Naturbild, 21 (top), Dorling Kindersley Ltd, 21 (bottom); Newscom/Dorling Kindersley, 20 (b), 25 (b); Shutterstock: ARTSILENSE, 26 (b), Aleksandra Dabrowa, 17 (t), Alena Kazlouskaya, 22 (b), Best dog photo, 10 (t), Bildagentur Zoonar GmbH, 8 (t), Capture Light, 12 (t), Csanad Kiss, 19 (b), cynoclub, 6 (t), 10 (b), 11 (b), Eric Isselee, cover (left), 6 (b), 7(b), 8 (b), 9 (b), 13 (b), 14 (b), 16 (b), 17 (b), 18 (b), 29 (t), GroanGarbu, 19 (t), HelenaQueen, 27 (b), Igor Marx, backcover, Jagodka, 24 (b), JP Chretien, 9 (t), Julia Remezova, 7 (t), Kachalkkina, 26 (t), Ksenia Raykova, 13 (t), Lee319, 11 (t), 24 (t), Lenkadan, 14 (t), Liliya Kulianionak, 27 (t), LSphotoCZ, 1, magdanphoto, 12 (b), Marcel Jancovic, 20 (t), Mikkel Bigandt, cover (top right), 4-5, miroslavmisiura, cover (bottom right), Nikolai Tsvetkov, 15, Sbolotova, 23 (t), Scandphoto, 16 (t), Schubbel, 18 (t), Susan Schmitz, 23 (b), 29 (b), Svetlana Valoueva, 22 (t); Superstock/Juniors, 25 (t)

Printed and bound in the United Kingdom.

FUN FACT

The Kennel Club was founded in 1873. The club is the largest dog registration database in the United Kingdom.

Australian Cattle Dog

FUN FACT

The Australian Cattle Dog is also known as the Australian Heeler.

Appearance:
Height: 43 to 51 centimetres (17 to 20 inches)
Weight: 14 to 20 kilograms (30 to 45 pounds)

Australian Cattle Dogs have a short double coat. It comes in either blue, blue speckle or red speckle. Some dogs have dark fur around one or both eyes. This marking makes it look like the dog is wearing a mask.

Personality: Australian Cattle Dogs make loving and loyal pets. They can be wary of strangers though. When they work as cattle herders, Australian Cattle Dogs are determined and courageous.

Breed Background: The breed was developed by carefully crossing the Dingo, the Kelpie, the Dalmatian and the Bull Terrier.

Country of Origin: Australia

Training Notes: Australian Cattle Dogs are smart and highly trainable. They respond especially well to rewards. Some owners train Australian Cattle Dogs for performance events, such as herding or **agility** competitions.

Care Notes: Australian Cattle Dogs can make great pets for the right people. Owners should be prepared to provide plenty of activity though. The breed needs two to three hours of exercise each day.

Australian Shepherd

Appearance:

Height: 46 to 58 centimetres (18 to 23 inches)
Weight: 18 to 29 kilograms (40 to 65 pounds)

The Australian Shepherd has medium-length fur. Many Australian Shepherds are merles, which means that the coat has a mixture of dark patches and lighter markings.

Personality: Australian Shepherds have strong personalities. Bred to herd sheep, they can be pushy pets. Some have even been known to try to herd children.

Country of Origin:

United States

Training Notes:

Australian Shepherds are highly intelligent and eager to please their owners. Positive training methods, such as treats and lots of praise, work best with this breed.

Care Notes: Although the Australian Shepherd's coat is medium-length, this breed doesn't need a lot of grooming. Regular brushing and occasional baths are usually enough to keep this dog clean and comfortable.

FUN FACT

After World War II (1939–1945), the Australian Shepherd's popularity skyrocketed when these dogs were shown in many films, on television and in rodeos and horse shows.

FAMOUS DOGS

The main character of the children's book *Henry the Dog with No Tail* is an Australian Shepherd. These dogs do have tails. They are just naturally short.

Bearded Collie

Appearance:

Height: 51 to 56 centmetres (20 to 22 inches)
Weight: 20 to 25 kilograms (45 to 55 pounds)

Bearded Collie puppies are born with a mixture of dark and white fur. As they move into adulthood, the darker colour lightens. Bearded Collies are often confused with Old English Sheepdogs. A Bearded Collie has a much longer tail, however.

Personality: Owners describe the Bearded Collie's personality as energetic and lively. Bearded Collies also love kids, but they can be a bit too rough for small children.

FUN FACT

The Bearded Collie is also known as the Mountain Collie or the Hairy Mou'ed Collie.

FAMOUS DOGS

The title role in the 2006 film *The Shaggy Dog* was played by a Bearded Collie.

Country of Origin:
Scotland

Training Notes:
Bearded Collies are strong-willed dogs. They need early training with **socialization**. This means meeting new people and other animals.

Care Notes: This long-haired breed needs a fair amount of grooming. Weekly brushing keeps tangles from forming. The breed also needs a bath every six to eight weeks.

Beauceron

Appearance:
Height: 63 to 70 centimetres (25 to 28 inches)
Weight: 29 to 39 kilograms (65 to 85 pounds)

The Beauceron has a short, smooth coat. The hair is slightly longer on the dog's neck, tail and backside. Most Beaucerons are black and tan. Some also have grey patches.

Personality: This devoted breed will work hard to please its owner. Beaucerons also have a strong **instinct** to protect their families.

Breed Background: Like many herding dogs, Beaucerons were developed to drive sheep and cattle. The Beauceron originated from the French Plains of Beauce.

Country of Origin: France

Training Notes: Training this intelligent breed is easy but important. Owners who do not properly train their Beaucerons can end up with a domineering pet.

Care Notes: Beaucerons are happiest when they have a purpose. These active dogs need to exercise both their bodies and their brains regularly. Organized activities, such as agility, are ideal for this breed.

FUN FACT

The French also refer to this breed as *Bas Rouge*, which means Red Stockings.

Belgian Shepherd Dog (Groenendael)

Appearance:
Height: 56 to 66 centimetres (22 to 26 inches)
Weight: 18 to 34 kilograms (40 to 75 pounds)

The Groenendael has long, black hair. Some dogs have a black coat with white patches. This breed's double coat is shorter on its head, ears and lower legs.

Personality:
Groenendaels can make confident, devoted companions. Groenendaels love to feel like they have a purpose or job to do.

Breed Background:
The four varieties of Belgian Shepherd Dogs are all named according to their Belgian region of origin. Professor Adolphe Reul of the Belgian Veterinary School named them.

Country of Origin: Belgium

Training Notes:
Similar to the Malinois, the Groenendael needs early training. These dogs are smart and quick learners. They are also commonly trained in the USA as police or military dogs or for search-and-rescue work.

Care Notes:
The Groenendael sheds year-round. It needs to be brushed weekly. This dog also needs adequate exercise, both mental and physical.

FUN FACT
During World War I (1914–1918), Belgian Sheepdogs worked on the battlefields as message carriers and ambulance dogs.

Belgian Shepherd Dog (Malinois)

Appearance:

Height: 56 to 66 centimetres (22 to 26 inches)
Weight: 27 to 29 kilograms (60 to 65 pounds)

The Malinois (MAL-in-wah) has a black muzzle and ears. Its main coat colour is a shade of red, **fawn** or grey.

Personality: This breed loves its human family. It takes time to warm up to strangers, however. The Belgian Malinois does well with older children.

Breed Background: The Belgian Malinois was developed as a sheepherder. Today members of this breed are best known for their work as police and military dogs.

Country of Origin: Belgium

Training Notes: The Belgian Malinois needs consistent training. Pups especially need socialization during their first six months of life.

Care Notes: The Mal's short coat makes grooming a simple task. These dogs do shed though. Regular brushing can help keep dead hair off carpets and furniture.

FUN FACT

The Belgian Malinois often runs in large circles. This habit comes from the breed's herding instinct.

Bergamasco

Appearance:
Height: 56 to 62 centimetres (22 to 25 inches)
Weight: 26 to 38 kilograms (57 to 84 pounds)

The Bergamasco has a long, harsh coat. The hair varies in colour from grey to black. Looking rather messy, the hair falls across the dog's eyes. It actually protects the animal's sight, though. This herding dog works high in the mountains where the sun glares off the snow.

Personality: The Bergamasco is known for its loyalty and love of children. These rare dogs make excellent watchdogs and family pets. They have a strong protective instinct.

Country of Origin: Italy

Training Notes: This smart breed has a strong personality. It needs an owner who is willing to put time and effort into training. Since most Bergamascos are wary of strangers, early socialization is also important.

Care Notes: The Bergamasco's heavy coat makes it a poor match for owners in warmer climates. These dogs thrive in cooler areas. A Bergamasco needs lots of exercise and prefers a countryside environment.

FUN FACT

When this breed is about a year old, a groomer should section its rough hair into cords. The process takes a lot of time. It never has to be done again, though.

Border Collie

Appearance:

Height: 46 to 58 centimetres (18 to 23 inches)
Weight: 14 to 20 kilograms (30 to 45 pounds)

Border Collies come in a variety of colours and patterns. A Border Collie can have a medium-length coat or a short, smooth coat. Common colours for Border Collies are black and white, but there are 50 colour variations.

Personality: Border Collies are best known for their intelligence and high energy. Due to their tendency to herd, Border Collies do best with older children.

Breed Background: The Border Collie is named for its area of origin. This dog was developed between England, Scotland and Wales and was used for working sheep in the hills and mountains.

Country of Origin: United Kingdom

Training Notes: If not properly trained, these dogs can become destructive. Early socialization and **crate** training are important for Border Collies. These dogs can also be trained for mountain rescue work.

Care Notes: Border Collies need a lot of physical exercise. They also require mental **stimulation**. Canine sports, such as fetch, can help satisfy both these needs.

FUN FACT

A herding Border Collie often walks in a crouched position. He looks like a cat hunting prey when he does this.

13

Briard

Appearance:

Height: 56 to 69 centimetres (22 to 27 inches)
Weight: 23 to 45 kilograms (50 to 100 pounds)

The Briard has long fur covering its body and face, varying in shades of blacks and fawn. These dogs are also known for having double **dewclaws** on the hind legs.

FUN FACT

Briards are sometimes used by armies as pack dogs, among other duties.

Personality: Briards make wonderful family pets. They are loyal, love kids and want to be part of all household activities. Briards love to engage in games.

Country of Origin: France

Training Notes: Briards are very independent, so owners need patience when teaching this breed commands. These dogs tend to be suspicious of strangers, so early socialization is important.

Care Notes: Briard owners must be willing to brush their dogs every other day. Tangles form quickly in this breed's long hair.

Collie (Rough)

Appearance:
Height: 51 to 61 centimetres (20 to 24 inches)
Weight: 23 to 34 kilograms (50 to 75 pounds)

Collies come in a variety of colours, including Sable and white, tricolour and Blue Merle. Many Collies have long, thick double coats, such as the Rough Collie. Other members of the breed have shorter, smooth coats.

Personality: Collies are known for their extreme companionship. Though independent, they share a deep bond with their human family members. Collies are good with children and other dogs.

Breed Background: The Collie's self-direction was considered a plus in its development. These herding dogs didn't just follow commands – they thought for themselves.

Country of Origin: Scotland

Training Notes: Collies are intelligent and easily trained. They are good listeners too. Gentle, positive training works best with these dogs.

Care Notes: A Collie doesn't demand a lot of exercise, but care should be taken to stop him from putting on too much extra weight. This dog's long hair should be brushed frequently to keep him looking his best.

FUN FACT

Millionaire banker J.P. Morgan bought a champion Collie in 1904. He paid £2,800 for the dog named Wishaw Clinker. Today that would be like spending £69,000 on a Collie.

Finnish Lapphund

Appearance:

Height: 44 to 49 centimetres (18 to 19 inches)
Weight: 15 to 24 kilograms (33 to 53 pounds)

The Finnish Lapphund comes in many colours. The most common are black and brown. Lappies, as they are sometimes called, can also have tan or white markings. The breed's long double coat protects it from the cold.

Personality: Many people see the Finnish Lapphund as the perfect pet. Lappies are calm and friendly with people. Their gentle **temperament** makes them great matches for families with kids.

Breed Background: The Finnish Lapphund was developed for hard work in cold temperatures, such as herding reindeer.

Country of Origin: Finland

Training Notes: The Finnish Lapphund is eager to learn and quick to train. When properly trained, these dogs get along well with other animals.

Care Notes: This breed is born with a soft coat that requires a lot of grooming. As the dog gets older, the coat becomes rougher. Weekly brushings will help keep a Lapphund's coat looking its best.

FUN FACT

Finnish Lapphunds were first bred to be dark-coloured so they would stand out in the snow.

German Shepherd Dog

Appearance:

Height: 58 to 63 centimetres (23 to 25 inches)
Weight: 34 to 43 kilograms (75 to 95 pounds)

German Shepherd Dogs are one of the most recognizable breeds. Their coats come in a wide range of colours and patterns. Most members of the breed have a black saddle with gold or tan hair on other parts of the body.

Personality: German Shepherds are loyal animals and make good family pets. They are known for calmly greeting people and for being well-behaved if properly trained.

Country of Origin: Germany

Training Notes: The German Shepherd is considered one of the smartest dog breeds. Training this breed is easy. An untrained German Shepherd, however, can be mischievous. Its bite is stronger than nearly all other dog breeds'.

Care Notes: Grooming a German Shepherd Dog isn't difficult. The breed does shed heavily though. Regular brushing can keep loose hair off owners and their belongings.

FUN FACT

German Shepherd Dogs are frequently used by police and the military. During World War I (1914–1918), over 48,000 German Shepherds were enlisted in the German army.

FAMOUS DOGS

A German Shepherd called Rin Tin Tin appeared in silent films in the 1920s. The character would later be played by two of the original dog's **descendants** on television.

Hungarian Kuvasz

FUN FACT

Although the Kuvasz is pure white in colous, his skin is highly pigmented with patches of grey.

Appearance:

Height: 66 to 75 centimetres (26 to 30 inches)
Weight: 30 to 52 kilograms (66 to 115 pounds)

The Kuvasz has a slightly wavy double coat. The fur is typically short and smooth on his head, muzzle and ears and fine and woolly on the undercoat. The Kuvasz is pure white in colour.

Personality: The Kuvasz is a devoted and gentle companion dog and is suitable as a family pet. This breed is known for its patience. However, sometimes a Kuvasz is wary of strangers.

Breed Background: It is believed that the Kuvasz played an important part in the history of kingdoms and empires that flourished throughout Europe five to eight centuries ago.

Country of Origin: Hungary

Training Notes: The Kuvasz needs a firm hand with training, coupled with attention and companionship in order to properly socialize him in the home.

Care Notes: Because these dogs are natural herders, they should be kept in a fenced area for their protection. His wavy, thick coat can withstand extreme cold weather, and it should be brushed reguarly.

Hungarian Puli

Appearance:

Height: 37 to 44 centimetres (15 to 18 inches)
Weight: 10 to 15 kilograms (22 to 33 pounds)

The Hungarian Puli stands out in any crowd. Its corded fur makes the dog look like a giant mop. These cords protect the dog from harsh weather. Though some dogs are white or grey, most members of this breed are black.

Personality: Pulik, the plural of Puli, are quite lively. They love being the centre of attention. They can make good pets for people with older children. They may be wary of strangers though.

FUN FACT

The Pulik, or Drovers, have been an essential part of the lives of Hungarian shepherds for more than a century.

Country of Origin: Hungary

Training Notes:
Pulik are highly intelligent and trainable. They do best when training begins early and remains consistent throughout adulthood.

Care Notes: Pulik are active animals and need daily exercise. Grooming them also takes effort and time. It can take an entire day for a dog to fully dry from a bath.

Komondor

Appearance:
Height: 60 to 80 centimetres (24 to 32 inches)
Weight: 36 to 61 kilograms (80 to 135 pounds)

The Komondor's hair clings together like tassels, giving it a corded appearance. But underneath those white tassels is one strong and powerful animal. The dog's coat alone can weigh 7 kilograms (15 pounds)!

Personality: The Komondor is not overly affectionate. It is an excellent guard dog and is highly protective of its human family members. This breed has even been known to protect other animals in its household.

Country of Origin: Hungary

Training Notes: This breed can be independent and stubborn, so owners should begin training a Komondor at a young age.

Care Notes: Owners should learn how to care for a Komondor's coat from an experienced breeder or groomer. These dogs need a fair amount of playtime and exercise, and plenty of countryside in which to roam.

FUN FACT

It is belived that he Komondor has been native to Hungary, a sheep and cattle country, longer than any other Pastoral breed.

Norwegian Buhund

Appearance:

Height: 41 to 45 centimetres (16 to 18 inches)
Weight: 12 to 18 kilograms (26 to 40 pounds)

The Norwegian Buhund comes in four colours: wheaten, which is yellow-brown, black, red and wolf-sable. A Buhund may also have a black mask or white markings.

Personality: This fearless, friendly breed stands out for its strong desire to please its owners. The Norwegian Buhund loves people, including children.

Breed Background:
The Buhund is a Spitz breed. Spitz dogs all descended from dogs in the Arctic region. A Spitz has dense fur, pointed ears and a pointed snout.

Country of Origin: Norway

Training Notes: The Buhund can be independent, but this dog learns quickly. Basic **obedience** and socialization training is also important from a young age.

Care Notes: This breed has a lot of energy. A Norwegian Buhund must run and play each day. Its coat is easy to care for, requiring occasional brushing and bathing.

FUN FACT

Bu in Norwegian means "homestead", so *Buhund* is the "dog found on the homestead or farm".

Old English Sheepdog

FUN FACT

The Old English Sheepdog has a unique **gait**. It runs much the same way a bear does.

FAMOUS DOGS

In the Disney cartoon *The Little Mermaid*, Prince Eric owns an Old English Sheepdog named Max.

Appearance:

Height: 56 to 61 centimetres (22 to 24 inches)
Weight: 27 to 41 kilograms (60 to 90 pounds)

The first thing anyone notices about the Old English Sheepdog is its wild, fluffy coat. Although it comes in several colours, the hair is usually grey, grizzle or blue.

Personality: This breed is known for its hoarse bark. Because these dogs are so big, kids may try to ride them. This isn't safe for either the child or the dog. As long as kids understand how to properly treat this friendly animal, an Old English Sheepdog can make a great family pet.

Country of Origin: England

Training Notes: Obedience training is a must, due to the breed's large size and level of energy. But do not overwork an Old English Sheepdog. Because bone growth continues for the first year and a half of their lives, it is more prone to injury during early training.

Care Notes: Old English Sheepdogs need lots of care and attention. Owners must spend about three to four hours each week on grooming. The energetic breed also needs about two hours of exercise each day.

Samoyed

Appearance:
Height: 46 to 56 centimetres (18 to 22 inches)
Weight: 16 to 29 kilograms (35 to 65 pounds)

The Samoyed's fluffy, white coat makes it easy to distinguish from other breeds. These dogs also look like they are smiling.

Personality: What sets this dog apart from other breeds most is its personality. Samoyeds are highly vocal. They tend to bark, howl and even seem to sing. A Sammie's singing sounds like varying pitches of prolonged howling.

Country of Origin: Russia

Training Notes: Samoyeds need training because of their high energy level. Excited dogs can be disobedient.

Care Notes: Samoyeds do not want to be inside all the time. They love spending time outdoors, especially in the snow. Their long coats need to be brushed weekly.

FUN FACT
Samoyeds were not always pure white. When Samoyeds were first brought to Britain, explorers described these dogs as being both black and white.

Shetland Sheepdog

Appearance:

Height: 35 to 37 centimetres (14 to 15 inches)
Weight: roughly 9 kilograms (20 pounds)

Shetland Sheepdogs have long double coats. They come in a variety of colours. Sable, tricolour, blue merle, black and white and white are among the most popular.

Personality: Shetland Sheepdogs are affectionate and responsive to their owners. However, sometimes Shetlanders, as they are often called, are wary of strangers.

Breed Background: The breed was developed on the Shetland Islands northeast of Scotland.

Country of Origin: Scotland

Training Notes: Shetlanders are among the smartest dog breeds and are easy to train. Shetlanders may bark and try to herd people. Basic socialization and command training should begin early on.

Care Notes: Shetlanders have a lot of energy. They like to play and tend to bark frequently. Active families are often the best matches for these dogs. Shetlanders are heavy shedders. Regular brushing is important. Brushing also helps prevents **mats**, which can cause skin problems in this breed.

FUN FACT

A dog called Loggie was the first Shetlander to appear at Crufts in 1906. Crufts is the world's largest dog show, held annually in the UK.

Swedish Vallhund

Appearance:

Height: 31 to 35 centimetres (12 to 14 inches)
Weight: 11 to 16 kilograms (25 to 35 pounds)

The Swedish Vallhund's low body, short coat and perky ears make it look like a Corgi. These dogs come in combinations of grey, red or yellow. White markings are also common on Swedish Vallhunds.

Personality: The Swedish Vallhund enjoys being on the go. These dogs are ideal for active people and will take all the exercise given. They are also friendly, alert and excellent guard dogs.

Country of Origin: Sweden

Training Notes: Swedish Vallhunds are easy to train. It is important to keep the tone positive though. This breed does not respond well to loud voices.

Care Notes: The Swedish Vallhund needs a lot of exercise. The breed loves long walks. Owners can also take this breed along when hiking. Its short coat requires occasional brushing and bathing.

FUN FACT

The Swedish Vallhund is also called the Swedish Cattle Dog.

Welsh Corgi (Cardigan)

Appearance:

Height: 25 to 33 centimetres (10 to 13 inches)
Weight: 11 to 17 kilograms (25 to 38 pounds)

The Cardigan Welsh Corgi stands low to the ground. While not tall, the Corgi is definitely long. They measure roughly 1 metre (3.3 feet) from nose to tail. The Cardigan's coat is short and **weatherproof**.

Personality: The Cardigan is a small dog with a big personality. It is driven and determined. It gets along well with older kids and makes a pleasant pet. It may try to herd young children, however.

Country of Origin: Wales

Training Notes: Cardigans are smart and easily trained. They are natural guardians, so socialization is important during early training.

Care Notes: A Corgi has more back problems than many other breeds due to its long, low back. Owners should not allow a Corgi to jump off a bed or other furniture. For exercise, a Corgi loves daily walks. Its short coat should be groomed regularly.

FUN FACT

The Cardigan's low height is helpful in herding. If a cow tries to kick the animal, chances are good that its hoof will go right over this dog's body!

Welsh Corgi (Pembroke)

Appearance:

Height: 25 to 30 centimetres (10 to 12 inches)
Weight: up to 12 kilograms (26 pounds)

The Pembroke's body is about one and a half times as long as it is tall. He is a double-coated breed. The inner coat is short and thick with longer, coarser hair over it.

Personality: The Pembroke has a lot of confidence for such a little dog. Perhaps that is why this breed was used to herd cattle. These dogs love their family members and make great pets though.

Country of Origin: Wales

Training Notes: This smart breed is eager to learn new things and to please its owner. Pembrokes also respond well to mental challenges, such as playing   fetch.

Care Notes:

Pembrokes should be kept on a sensible canine diet. This breed is prone to weight gain if owners overfeed their dogs. Exercise is also important for this lively breed.

FUN FACT

The easiest way to tell the difference between this breed and the Cardigan is looking at their tails – the Pembroke has a much shorter, or docked, tail.

FAMOUS DOGS

Great Britain's Queen Elizabeth II has owned more than 30 Pembrokes during her reign.

Belgian Shepherd Dog (Tervueren)

Appearance:
  Height: 56 to 66 centimetres (22 to 26 inches)
  Weight: 26 to 42 kilograms (57 to 93 pounds)
Known for: being closely related to the Belgian Sheepdog
Country of Origin: Belgium

....

Picardy Sheepdog

Appearance:
  Height: 55 to 65 centimetres (22 to 26 inches)
  Weight: 25 to 35 kilograms (55 to 77 pounds)
Known for: performing well in the show ring
Country of Origin: France

....

Polish Lowland Sheepdog ▶

Appearance:
  Height: 42 to 50 centimetres (17 to 20 inches)
  Weight: 22 to 30 kilograms (49 to 66 pounds)
Known for: fearlessly protecting their flocks from predators
Country of Origin: Poland

....

Pyrenean Sheepdog (Long Haired) ▼

Appearance:
   Height: 40 to 48 centimetres (16 to 19 inches)
   Weight: 20 to 28 kilograms (44 to 62 pounds)
Known for: living in the Pyrenees Mountains
   for centuries
Countries of Origin: France and Spain

Glossary

agility ability to move fast and easily

crate plastic or metal pen or kennel; used for housetraining and transporting dogs in the car

descendant person or animal who comes from a particular group of ancestors

dewclaw functionless claw present in some dogs, not reaching the ground while walking

fawn light brown colour

gait way of walking

instinct behaviour that is natural rather than learned

mat thick, tangled mass of hair

obedience obeying rules and commands

socialize train to get along with people and other dogs

stimulate encourage interest or activity in a person or animal

temperament combination of an animal's behaviour and personality; the way an animal usually acts or responds to situations shows its temperament

weatherproof able to withstand exposure to all kinds of weather

Read more

Caring for Dogs and Puppies (Battersea Dogs & Cats Home Pet Care Guides), Ben Hubbard (Franklin Watts, 2015)

Everything Dogs (National Geographic for Kids), Becky Baines (National Geographic, 2012)

Looking After Dogs and Puppies (Pet Guides), Katharine Starke (Usborne Publishing Ltd, 2013)

Websites

http://animals.nationalgeographic.com/animals/mammals/domestic-dog/
Learn all about domestic dogs through photos, videos, facts and more on this National Geographic website.

www.ykc.org.uk/
Become a member of the Young Kennel Club and discover lots of different events you and your dog can attend, including training and fun agility days.

Index